Old Grand Rapids

A PICTURE STORY
of OLD CONDITIONS

MR. AND MRS. LOUIS CAMPAU
Founders of Our City

*Intended only as supplementary to
the local histories, so well written
by Albert Baxter and others*

Geo. E. Fitch

1925

ISBN 0-9617706-0-0

Revised and Updated by James VanVulpen and Gordon Olson

*T*HE collecting of these old pictures has been interesting on account of the difficulty of securing them. Some have been sent me from distant states, and many a clue has been followed with no resulting picture.

Photography was unknown here until our city was twenty years of age.

The earliest street scene, taken with a glass plate and paper print, was in 1857—and most of these pictures were taken with the "wet plate" made by the photographer and exposed while still wet.

Before 1857, I show a daguerreotype taken on a metal plate—in 1852—as well as several sketches and paintings.

Disastrous fires between 1868 and 1873 burned much of our down town section. Many of the old scenes were never photographed and doubtless many photographs were not preserved.

I consider myself fortunate in collecting as many as I have and take pleasure in putting them in more permanent form for others to examine.

I have arranged the views as nearly as possible as you would see them in a ramble around the old town.

If you get lost on the circuit telephone me.

GEO. E. FITCH

Introduction to Second Edition

by James VanVulpen

GEORGE EVERETT FITCH (1868-1941) came naturally to his lifelong fascination with the history of Grand Rapids. His grandfather, Professor Franklin Everett, was one of West Michigan's foremost local historians, whose 1878 masterpiece, *Memorials of the Grand River Valley*, was the earliest large-scale study of the region. For the first 25 years of his life, young George absorbed a deep sense of the past from his close relationship with the older man.

Following his graduation from Central High School in 1888 and the University of Michigan in 1892, Fitch's business career was a brief one. Two years as a partner in the Valley City Spring Bed Company ended with that firm's failure during the devastating depression of the mid-1890s. During the rest of his life, he dabbled in real estate sales, but many city directories over the years list no occupation for him at all. Apparently the family inheritance sufficed to support him comfortably and to provide for his unmarried sister, Louise.

As a bachelor "gentleman of leisure" in early 20th-century Grand Rapids, Fitch had ample time to pursue his hobbies. He was an avid canoeist during his vigorous years, exploring almost every navigable waterway in lower Michigan. He was an enthusiastic amateur photographer and a charter member of the local camera club. But George E. Fitch was best known by his home town for his general knowledge of its days gone by and for his efforts as a collector of the pictorial record of those days.

Even though an interest in Grand Rapids' history began quite early in the town's existence, with articles by Professor Everett and others appearing in newspapers during the 1850s, a corresponding interest in saving pictorial evidence seems not to have developed until much later. As his grandfather had done in amassing pioneer lore, Fitch assembled the earliest, and easily the finest, collection of 19th-century Grand Rapids photos and drawings. That collection now reposes in the Public Library's Michigan Room. For years Fitch was much in demand around the city for lantern slide shows and lectures on his pet subject. Finally, wishing to add his bit to the permanent record for posterity, he gathered the choicest of his pictures, wrote brief explanations of them, and published in late 1925 at his own expense this book, *Old Grand Rapids.*

Now, more than 60 years since the volume's first appearance, the Grand Rapids Historical Society is proud to issue this second edition of a landmark work. Modern readers, perhaps even more than the book's first audience, will delight in its special quality of allowing them to look back through time at an earlier Grand Rapids of which much has vanished since 1925. Furthermore, it seemed appropriate to the Society's publication committee that Fitch's good work be expanded. The first section of this edition faithfully reproduces his original volume. Following that is a brief list of updates relating the author's 1925 references to the present, along with corrections of some facts and dates based on more recent research into primary sources, many of which were unavailable to Fitch. Section two, compiled by City Historian Gordon Olson, forms a 20th-century counterpart to Fitch's "ramble" around the 19th-century city. *Old Grand Rapids* thus becomes, in effect, a new pictorial history based on the best resources, both old and new.

But after all, as one reading will prove, a picture may indeed be worth a thousand words. Just turn the page and hop aboard the "time machine." You're in for a wonderful trip.

MONROE STREET 94 years ago—This sketch was made in 1831 by one of the Baptist missionaries. You are on the old Indian Trail leading down to Louis Campau's Trading Post—the three log cabins at the right. The Baptist Mission buildings show across the river, and Chief Noonday's hut at the left.

THE same view today. You would be standing in front of Herpolsheimer's, looking at the Pantlind Hotel as shown in the picture below, but even that is not a modern picture, as Sweet's Hotel is still in evidence, and Herpolsheimer has now a glass and metal sidewalk awning.

An Early Map Obtained from the City Engineer's Office May Help Us to Understand a Few Kinks in Our Downtown Streets

*L*OUIS Campau located here in 1826 as Indian Trader, but the land was not open for Government entry till 1831. By that time other men were looking over the prospect—among them Lucius Lyon, who saw the advantage of the land at the foot of the rapids and head of possible navigation. Lucius Lyon and John Mullett were the surveyors of this land for the government. It turned out to be almost a race to the Land Entry Office (at either Battle Creek or Kalamazoo)—and Campau won out by only a few hours. He secured his forty acres and soon platted as shown in the central portion of the accompanying map—bounded by Fulton Street, Division Street, the river, and, on the north, a line halfway between Lyon and Pearl Streets. Lucius Lyon, failing to get this location, took the next land to the north—now known as Kent Plat.

Campau laid out Monroe Street on the old Indian Trail leading down to his Trading Post at Lock Street—where the Interurban Station now stands. Also notice the names of Water, Justice, Greenwich, and Official Streets and the angle at which Monroe ran into Pearl. Campau's ire was up against Lyon for nearly undermining his plans and so platted a continuous row of lots along the north edge, numbered from 1 to 16 on the map—and then told Lyon that he would allow no street access to his plat through the row. "To come in my plat you must come around by Division Street".

He sold Lots Nos. 1 and 2 to a Mr. Wadsworth under a pledge to put up a mill and other buildings. To take advantage of the current for power, Wadsworth built the mill extending over the shore and then, not needing all the land, sold a strip to Lyon who opened up Canal Street to Pearl—but not in line with Monroe Street. This increased the feeling between Lyon and Campau and no other street access was possible so Lyon platted another bank of lots back to back— as shown on the map—and laid out Canal Street, Kent, Ottawa, and Ionia, at about equal distances.

Let us see what happened as a result of this war. Kent Street never has been opened to Pearl—although proceedings have been started four or five times to condemn for that purpose. Ottawa Street, eventually connected with Justice Street in 1863, does so at an angle in front of Klingman's Furniture Building. Ionia Street, opposite the City Hall and Post Office, does not line up by twelve or fifteen feet—and had it not been for that jog at the foot of the street we should never have had Campau Square (or is it a triangle?).

On the map, please notice the locks at the foot of the canal and the Basin off the canal where boats were to load and unload on their way up or down the river. Notice that Fountain Street extended east only to Ransom. Fulton Street Park was the Court House Square, Louis Street was named after Campau, but Campau Street at that time was only a part of the Indian Camping Ground on the Island.

Many changes have occurred to alter the appearance of our city's geography. Prospect Hill was a hard clay knoll extending from Division and Monroe Streets down along Monroe and north to the County Building at Crescent Street. Where it crossed Pearl Street, it was about forty feet above the river level. Lower Monroe and Canal Streets have been raised as much as seventeen feet to avoid flooding.

Several brooks ran to the river. One at Michigan from the old Arctic Spring. One from Fountain Street, which made a large pond at the Post Office Square, then ran under the City Hall and County Buildings, and then through another pond before reaching the river at Huron Street. Another brook started near Lake Avenue and Fulton, ran through the valley of Dudley Waters' yard, across to Washington Street and Island Street to the big swamp at the Union Station.

There were other brooks farther south, notably one from the big Penny Spring near the corner of Madison and Logan, that later was used by the Hydraulic Company for a water supply which was conducted to the city center by log pipes. The Four Islands in the river extending from Pearl to Wealthy, long since annexed to the eastern shore by filling in, were purchased from the Government by Campau in 1841, and two docks were located at Fulton Street and Pearl in the eastern channel.

An Early Map Obtained from City Engineer's Office

THIS is not a photograph, but a copy of a sketch made by Mr. Turner—both from description and memory—and gives us an idea how the city looked from Island No. 1 in 1834. Guild's house was built on the corner between Pearl and Monroe Streets—and "Prospect Hill" looms up just east.

To be correct, the water in the foreground should be much wider, as it would have required a long bridge span to cross it.

Many of our city streets are named in memory of the owner of the plat—such as Edmund B. Bostwick, Lucius Lyon, H. P. Bridge, James Scribner, Billius Stocking, and a hundred others.

Some street names have a special origin and significance.

Louis Campau's license to establish an Indian Trading Post and his entry of Government land closely coincide with Monroe's administration. It does not follow that Washington, Madison, and Jefferson are also presidential names, as Jefferson Morrison named two streets after himself and another in honor of his wife, Wealthy Morrison.

Fulton Street ran down to the dock behind Island No. 2 and was named about the time Fulton was being honored for developing the steamboat.

Division Street is a surveyor's division line between Sections 11 and 12.

Lock Street is beside the canal locks that were started but never completed.

College Avenue was the site of a college that was never built.

When Fountain Street extended only to Ransom on the east, a large spring and brook in the hillside at that point suggested the name.

A group of black cherry trees gave Cherry Street its name, while Island and Ferry Streets terminated at the Island and Ferry at the river.

Kent, Ottawa, and Ionia sound like three adjoining counties—Kent being named for Chancellor Kent of New York.

State Street is all that remains of the old State Road, all that part east of Madison being vacated in 1860.

In the very early days the northern portion of our city tried to be known as the Village of Kent, though there never was an incorporated village of that name. In the same way Campau's plat was named as Grand Rapids though the incorporation was much later.

A SKETCH of the islands in the river, made by Miss Mary Cuming in 1861. You are standing at the east end of Pearl Street bridge. The large sycamore tree stands in Campau Street in front of the jail. The islands beyond the tree form our City Market. At the left, you can see the boat landing at the foot of Fulton Street. These islands were the favorite camping ground for the Indians.

PEARL Street bridge was completed in 1858. An embankment across the east channel extended Pearl Street to the bridge.

This shows the head of Island No. 1.

The eastern bank of the river is today out in the middle of this span of the bridge.

THE old stone High School was built in 1849—on the site of the present Junior High School on Ransom Street at Lyon. 44 x 64 feet in size—of river stone—at a cost of about $2500.00. Taken down in 1867.

With Prof. Cheesboro's permission we will go up into the tower of this building and take the two views shown on the next page.

TAKEN from the tower of the old Stone School House.

Just over the many steeplets of the old Methodist Church you can see the white National Hotel—later the Morton. Also the round top Rink Building where Fulton Street touches the river. The Kennedy Livery on Fountain Street later became the Bell Telephone building. The tower of the Catholic Church shows on Monroe Street and the scaffolding is still up for the additions to St. Marks Church.

ANOTHER view taken in 1873 brings in the new Baptist Church, but the National Hotel is gone in the fire of September 20, 1872.

The Baptist Church in the view was just completed and was first occupied in 1873.

You can see the trees on Islands Nos. 3 and 4 in the river.

THE Swedenborgian Church Society was organized by Lucius Lyon who gave them a lot to build upon at the foot of Lyon Street hill at Division.

Building put up in 1852 but dissension in the church nearly broke up the society who had little use of the place.

Five other societies had their beginnings here—

Second Congregational	1852-56
Westminster Presbyterian	1861-65
Christian Reformed	1870-72
Free Will Baptist	1872-
Disciples	1875-87

Again used by Swedenborgians. Making six churches organized and the death of two in this building.

ST. Marks Church—first occupied in October, 1848. Erastus Hall was the first sexton and collector of pew rents for which he received $100.00 per year—he to furnish the heating and lights for the building. This view shows the building somewhat enlarged—in 1865.

If you will notice, the church had two front doors at that time.

The lady near the tree at the left moved during the taking of the photograph and you can see the fence through her hoop skirt.

METHODIST Church—corner stone laid 1868—southeast corner of Division and Fountain.

This photograph was taken before 1873 as the Baptist Church is not yet built.

ST. Marks First Church—built at the northwest corner of Crescent and Division—27 x 41 feet in size—cost $800.00—first used April, 1841. Later enlarged and moved to corner of Library and Division. Sold to the Baptists in 1848.

EAST end of Pearl Street about 1875. The old homes are still on Post Office Square, Daniel Tower occupying the first one at the left.

OUR first post office was at the Mission Station in 1832, but in 1834 Joel Guild's home was appointed. In 1836 it is said that the post office was in Darius Windsor's coat pocket.

The first real station was in the Eagle building, Lyon Street, in 1868, where it remained until this Government building was erected in 1879.

THE Universalist Church held their first meetings in the old Luce's Hall in 1858. Later, in 1868, they built this church—where the Chamber of Commerce Building is now located.

View in 1875.

THE Samuel Perkins home was one of the oldest landmarks to remain near the center of the city.

Mrs. Perkins moved into it as a bride in 1840 and remained there till her death 70 years later.

This corner was purchased for $200.00—and is about the same size as its next neighbor, The Michigan Trust Company.

View taken about 1915.

THIS view was taken in 1860 from the third floor of the old Irving Hall (now Boston Store)—looking over the small wooden buildings on Monroe Street—past the newly graded cut in Pearl Street—and shows Daniel Ball's home and Crescent Park in the distance.

The Daniel Ball house was built in 1850—removed in 1888. The house at the right edge of the view was the home of Wilder D. Foster.

This grading was done in 1857. Again graded deeper in 1865 as will show in another picture.

WHEN the big cut in Pearl left Daniel Ball's (later the Morton Home) high above the street, some attempt was made to make the place accessible by means of inclined drives and steps.

This view was after the second grading cut in 1865.

Later the Peninsular Club used this house for a while—but the last tenant before its removal in 1880 was the Truant School.

LOOKING down Pearl Street—1870. Crane's Museum of freaks, snakes, and whiskered ladies was located over Houseman and May's Clothing Store. The Lovett Block on the corner was not fully built, on top, and Borden's Store, known as the Tanner Taylor Corner, was still standing in the center of the Square.

In 1874 Canal Street grade was raised four feet and Sweet's Hotel elevated to match the new level.

The Lovett Block opposite was not raised, but another floor was built in four feet above the old—shortening the height of the first story.

Ottawa St. from Pearl to Monroe, 1865

THE heavy grading in Lyon, Pearl, and Ottawa Streets, through the hills, was completed in 1865—much of the dirt filling being used in the pond at the Post Office Square, the creek valley under the City Hall, and the Channel of the river east of Island No. 1 and No. 2.

This view shows the teams finishing the grade in Ottawa Street—beside the Michigan Trust Building.

The first grading in 1857 shows at the fence level.

This is our first view of St. Andrews Church. The old Stone Catholic, on Monroe Street.

HALDANE Home (now Michigan Trust) sold to the City for a City Hall site in 1872 for $11,000.00.

Used by the City for offices of Justices and Water Works until they moved to our present City Hall.

In 1878 a large bell was purchased (4000 pounds) and placed in a tower of wood for a fire alarm.

In 1882 they extended this tower to 208 feet above Canal Street and attempted to light the entire city by means of eight arc lights.

Haldane's cabinet shop on part of this lot in 1835 produced the first furniture made here—and it was the start out of which developed the Nelson-Matter Furniture Co.

This house was taken down in 1890.

THIS is the same view as on the opposite page as it looks today.

DR. Charles Shepard was the first to come and longest to remain of the old school family physicians.

Arrived in Grand Rapids October, 1835. Built this stone cottage on Prospect Hill in 1843 where it remained till 1890 (now Young & Chaffee's location on Ottawa St.).

Dr. Shepard opened the first drug store—which he later sold to L. D. Putnam.

The grading of Ottawa Street left this home about fifteen feet above the sidewalk.

A VIEW toward the hill—from between the Dr. Shepard and Robert's homes.

Hartman's big auditorium holding 3000 later occupied the space back of Dr. Shepard's home—and that too is gone.

Livery barns and small houses show where large buildings use every inch today.

THE National Hotel was built soon after the fire of 1855, this time four stories high and covering the entire lot. It had several proprietors before it was again burned on September 20, 1872.

The National, from its position, was fortunate in catching most of the old stage coach trade.

The old well remained at the corner in Ionia Street, but was covered with a curb and pump.

The Morton House was erected soon after the fire of '72.

THE OLD NATIONAL HOTEL.
Erected on the present site of the Morton House in 1835—Burned in 1855

The First Hotel on the Morton House Corner

THE Hinsdill House, renamed "The National" by Canton Smith, was built in 1835. Burned in '55.

It contained a ballroom on the second floor. In Ionia Street at the corner of the hotel was the stone well, forty feet deep and walled with stone. Windlass and buckets brought up the water and Wilder D. Foster furnished the tin cups.

Kalamazoo Coach

THREE or more routes of stage lines in 1850 to Lansing, Battle Creek and Kalamazoo. These were little better than square box farm wagons with or without seats and cover.

On the completion of the plank road to Kalamazoo a line of coaches was introduced and this shorter route captured nearly all of the trade for thirteen years until trains were running.

The first toll on the completion of the old plank road was taken in 1855.

This is the Kalamazoo coach taken at Plainwell.

A GLANCE up Monroe Street in 1864. Luce's Block at the right seems to be decorated as a part of the election campaign. If you were on the other side of the banner you could read

Lincoln and Johnson
Freedom and the Union

The old stone Catholic Church, built in 1849-50 is now West's Drug Store.

The old Congregational Church steeple shows at Division Street and one of the oil burning street lights shows up against the church.

The church and grounds were sold in 1872-73 to Moses V. Aldrich for $56,000.00 and the stone of the old church was used in the foundation of the new St. Andrews to follow.

VAN DRIELE had his Feed Store on the corner opposite the Morton for many years. The festoons on the building were part of the Centennial decorations—1876. Today we are watching the big Grand Rapids Trust Co. structure go up.

RICE and Moore for many years ran a grocery on the corner where the Grand Rapids Savings Bank now stands. The second floor was the first Police Headquarters—from 1871 to 1882 when they moved to the corner of Lyon and Campau Streets.

A VIEW down Monroe Street from the National Hotel balcony—1859.

The big Luce Block at the left was built in 1856 and the third and fourth floors west was Luce's Hall—which for many years was our most popular auditorium.

One block below you can see the sloping roof of the Rathbun.

Farthest west is a brick block built for Daniel Ball's Bank. This was enlarged later to make Sweet's Hotel.

The cobblestone pavement was new in '56.

IN this view Ottawa Street has not completed its grade and you can see the ascent toward the old hill.

Wells Bank once occupied the corner at Ottawa—later reopened by the Ellis Bank.

THIS is the earliest photograph taken on a glass negative of any local scene. Taken by Jim Keeney in 1857. Looking down Market Street. You can see the Eagle on the hotel sign and the words below: "Kalamazoo Stage Line".

Notice the two board sidewalks and residences—all at a lower level, as all have since been raised to the height of Monroe Street.

Jim Keeney bought out O. W. Horton's gallery in 1856—and sold back to him in 1858.

Up to 1857 only daguerreotypes and ambrotypes had been produced.

THE first hotel was the Eagle, built in 1834. The first story and a half house was several times enlarged. Burned in February, 1883, when the present brick hotel was erected.

The original building was begun by a Mr. J. S. Potter, but was completed by Louis Campau.

IN 1834 Louis Campau built a home on Monroe Street at Market and lived there till 1838—when it was raised and enlarged to make what was later the Rathbun House.

The stone addition at the back was built in 1846. The whole was torn down in 1885.

CAPTAIN Belknap in his valuable reminiscences explains the coinage of the term "Grab Corners".

In 1865, Lieut. Bob Wilson, returning from the war, took a job as reporter on the Daily Eagle. He cartooned, ridiculed and satirized the local conditions around our civic center till the public accepted the title and took steps to transform "Grab Corners" into "Campau Square"—at a cost of $50,000.00—1870.

A close-up view of the buildings just before removal from Campau Square—1873. The Stone Commercial Block was built in 1844, Crawford's checkered store was brilliant in its checks of many colors and the Taylor (later Borden) store on the corner was the last to be removed. Borden fought the condemnation proceedings but a mysterious fire broke out and firemen found their apparatus reluctant to do anything except save adjoining property.

A photograph taken a few months later. The old buildings in the Square are gone but the lines of the foundations in the ground still show —1873.

THE old hardware building was the farthest south of the four structures on the Square, as shown on the opposite page.

It stood partly behind the corner of Irving Hall block so the whole front could not be seen from up Monroe Street.

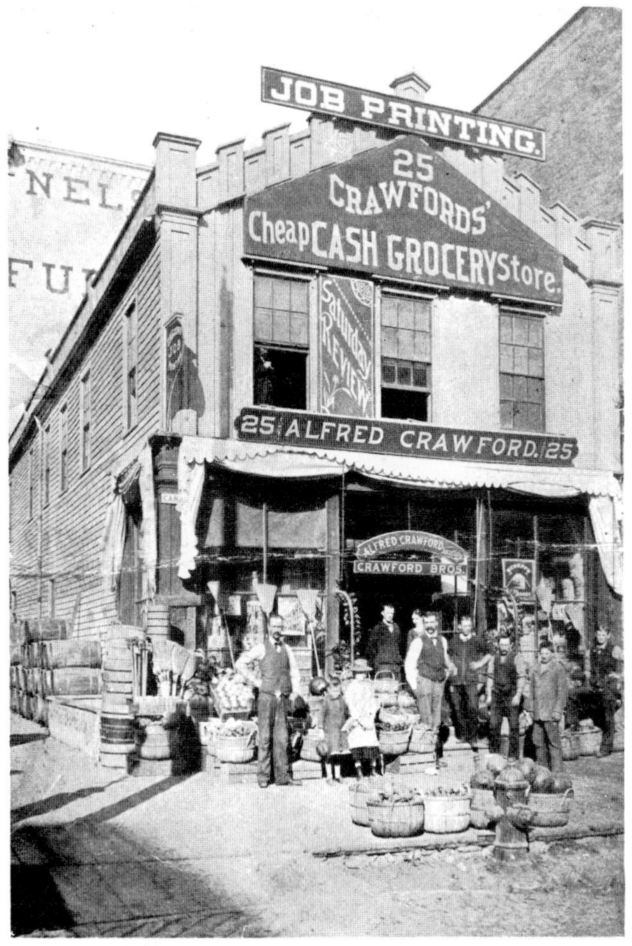

THE Crawford Grocery Store is best remembered in the old Checkered Store in the middle of Campau Square. When forced from there by the clearing out of the old row of buildings, we find him on the northwest corner of Lyon and Canal Streets where one of our big bank buildings now stands.

CAMPAU Square in 1852.   This was copied from a daguerreotype made by Proctor and Buel who had a gallery on the third floor of the Gunn Block, then known as Faneuil Hall.

From their front window you are looking down past the balcony of the old Rathbun (on the left).   Notice the wooden awnings over the three buildings in the Square and the town flag pole.

The Checkered Store was not yet so decorated—and Canal Street is several feet lower than Pearl.

No brick blocks are in the picture but Bridge Street bridge shows up well in the background.

Hall's Book Store, Joseph Martin's Grocery and Powers & Ball—Furniture, are the three buildings on Pearl Street.

The little, dark-front, one-story affair opposite the Rathbun (over on the right) is Guild's home made over into Wm. Fulton's meat market—with a swinging sign of a bull in front.   This was the first house built on the first lot Campau sold.   Campau asked Guild $25.00 a lot but as he bought two lots he closed the bargain at $45.00—the two lots now owned by the National City Bank.

DANIEL BALL'S BANK—now the Old National—was built in 1859, with McConnell's hardware as a neighbor, and the telegraph next. Express office in the rear. This building was enlarged to make Sweet's Hotel in 1868.

THIS view of Campau Square is from the same spot that the one on the opposite page was taken—but 73 years later.

THE West Side Volunteer Fire Co. posed for their photograph in the summer of 1860 in Campau Square.

Chas. Belknap is holding a trumpet at the extreme left. Wm. Hyde, foreman, has another trumpet and Ira Thompson stands behind him.

C. G. Utley is the boy mascot on the top of the machine and Wm. James, Abe Lawyer, Geo. Howland, Jos. Bennett, and E. G. D. Holden are standing at the right front—in that order.

Notice the two-wheel dray at the right edge of the picture.

The building at the extreme left is the Rathbun House. Then Barth's Variety Store (with the white sash), H. Leonard—Crockery next, while the hanging clock shows Chas. Bolza's Jewelry Store. He was killed in the Civil War.

Behind A. D. Rathbone on the sidewalk is Henry's Drug Store. Then the entrance to Irving Hall and Sears' Bakery—last, Irving Hall Block, torn down 1868. The street gas light was new in 1857.

A WOOD cut from an early sketch showing the same buildings as the photo on the opposite page.

The Gunn Block—at the corner of Market was built by Jacob Winsor, of river stone in 1844. It was called Faneuil Hall.

Notice the two little buildings at the left shown in the "Grab Corners" 1852 view two pages back.

The building at the right is "Irving Hall". Both of these "Halls" were early assembly places that went out of existence soon after Luce's Hall came in.

Irving Hall removed 1868.

LOOKING across Monroe Street from the Rathbun House in 1870, we can see some of the old wooden buildings still ornamenting the landscape.

Just opposite—read the sign over the door—
H. Leonard—Crockery

LOOKING up Canal Street from Pearl, in 1870.

The street car is waiting at the switch.

The two big blocks on the first corners at Lyon Street were both faced with Gypsum Plaster Rock.

Notice the numerous hitching posts at the left to tie the Fords, and the only wires on the pole at the left were the telegraph line.

LOOKING across the old east channel of the river to the new jail on Island No. 2—1872.

The filling up of the channel was begun in 1868 and the tail race for Butterworth & Lowe water wheel at the end of the canal shows in the center. The G. R. & I. is on a trestle to the island—and the mudhole in the foreground is the site of the Fourth National Bank, best known as the Tower Clock Building.

SWEET'S Hotel was built in 1868—opened in '69. In 1874 the building was raised to the new street grade—four feet higher.

PEARL Street bridge was the same type of construction as those at Bridge and Leonard Streets.

Pearl bridge was finished November, 1858. All three were purchased by the city and made free of toll in '73 and '74.

The iron bridge at Pearl Street was erected in 1886. Before bridges were built, for several summers wooden saw horses held up plank walkways across the river. During high water a ferry at Ferry Street was in operation.

In 1865, the soldiers returning from the war were given a dinner on this bridge.

In 1881, the first street electric arc lights were displayed here by the Wm. T. Powers Co.

They were building the Tower Clock building when this photo was taken.

OLD first D. & M. bridge built in 1858, replaced later by the iron girder spans.

The log booms in the river above the dam separated the supply of logs to the several mills.

THE big log jam. Unusual rains during June and July, 1883, made high water in the river. Lumbermen took advantage of it to float down their logs. A jam formed at the D. & M. bridge and the logs massed thirty feet deep and seven miles long.

July 26, 1883, the bridge gave way and 100,000,000 feet of logs, forced by the flood conditions, shot through town in less than two hours.

On their way they took down three railroad bridges and damaged the others.

BOTH views show the jam above the bridge. In the upper view you are looking over the bridge railing.

WHEN the pressure of the flood behind the mass of logs became too great, the central spans of the steel D. & M. bridge gave way and the logs started on their mad race through the city.

ONE of the spans of the G. R. & I. bridge taking a ride down stream.

But few of the logs reached Lake Michigan. The bayous and swamps of the lower river were filled and most of the logs failed to find their true owners.

THE earliest boat on the river was the Governor Mason in 1834.

Until the railroad arrived in 1858, all the heavy freight came by boat.

The Barrett was the last of a series of forty or more boats that ran the river. Years later we had two boats—the Grand and the Rapids—for one or two seasons, but navigation was too dead to revive.

THE greatest flood our city ever experienced was in February, 1838. The ice in the river broke up and jammed 30 feet high near Wealthy Avenue, and the ice and water flooded the city. Two river boats were caught in the jam. One—the Governor Mason, was forced inland to the corner of Island and Commerce (Spring) Sts. and had to be moved back to the river on rollers weeks later.

The other boat escaped the ice and unloaded a cargo of flour in the second story window of a warehouse on Market Street and then returned to the river by the way of Monroe and Pearl Streets.

AFTER the channel was filled in behind Islands 1 and 2, a canal and turn-basin were constructed behind Island 4. In this scene we are looking north, up the channel. The barn-like warehouse on the dock, which you can see over the boat, and the enlarged north end of the channel where the boats were swung around are both now covered up by the Island Park Ball Grounds.

A VIEW from the top of the old Gunn Block. We can see the top edge of the old Eagle Hotel and beyond a few of the warehouses along Waterloo Street and two of Daniel Ball's boats at landings on the other side of the river.

The G. R. & I. Railroad passes over to the island on a trestle and the upper ends of Islands Nos. 3 and 4 can be seen below.

A VIEW northward on Summit Street. The old round-top Rink building had a varied existence ending as the home of Ball's Buss Lines. It was removed to open Fulton Street to the river.

The Barnard House stands next north.

Taken about 1875.

THREE fire companies were organized in 1849-50, each having a hand-operated pump and all three a total length of 250 feet of copper riveted leather hose. The men received no salary and were fined 50c if they missed a fire.

The first steam pump arrived in 1865 under a citizens' protest against the unnecessary expense.

This is the Kent Street Company having their photo taken on the island, about 1865. Compay No. 2.

THIS view and the one below are taken from the same spot on the hill top—Summit Street. You can see the back and tower of the old Stone Church on Monroe St. Both views taken about 1870.

G. R. & I. Union Station was ready when their service started in 1870. All the clusters of small buildings between the station and Summit Street were known as Shantytown. Now all covered by tracks and warehouses.

DR. Alonzo Platt was one of the first physicians to locate here. He arrived in 1842 and built this stone cottage about 1850—which is now the site of the Cody Hotel.

He died in 1882, after forty years of practice. He and Dr. Chas. Shepard are remembered as the oldest family doctors.

LOUIS Campau built this church in 1837 for the Catholics and it was used by them for a few years. The Catholic Society was unable to buy it so in 1841 it was sold to the Congregational Society.

Burned November 26, 1872.

Corner of Division and Monroe—now the Porter Block.

The first big bell in town (1000 lbs.) was placed in this tower in 1842.

DR. Platt's home, built out to Division Street line for business purposes—1880.

Taken down to build the Cody.

You can still see the railing-top of the old stone cottage.

NO. 2 Primary School on South Division. Land cost $500.00 in 1861. Torn down 1884.

THE Kent County Agricultural Society held their first Fair at the west end of Bridge Street bridge, 1848—on the Court House Square, 1849—and for several years at the corner of Fulton and Jefferson Streets. In 1855 at the corner of Wealthy and Division, but in December, 1855, they purchased 40 acres south of Hall Street between Jefferson and Madison.

This is a corner of their main Art Hall on those grounds. Not having sufficient buildings, the apple and fruit display can be seen outdoors.

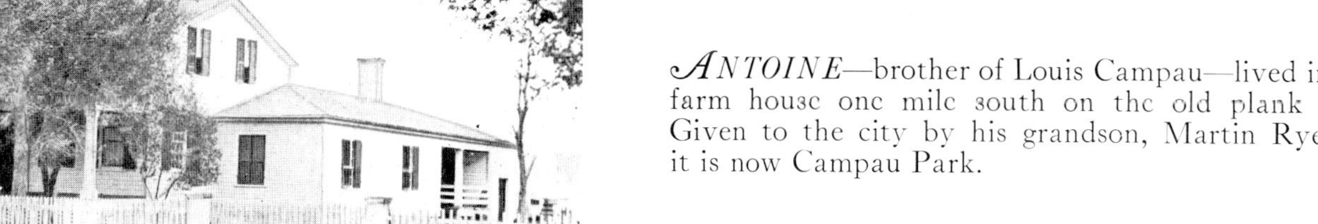

ANTOINE—brother of Louis Campau—lived in this farm house one mile south on the old plank road. Given to the city by his grandson, Martin Ryerson, it is now Campau Park.

A VIEW taken from the roof of the old Park Place—now the Herald Building.

Peck's Drug Store corner was just completed. The old stores were still on the Wenham Block corner and Boynton's street car tracks are shown on North Division Street.

COURT House Square had a $3000.00 Court Building 30 x 40 feet in 1838—burned in 1844. Replaced by a single room building costing $300.00.

Indian payments were made there and the first county fairs (1849-50) were held on the Square. A menagerie in 1850 and the first circus in town (June, 1858) used the Square and the rental was used for tree planting.

In 1860 the question of forbidding cattle or swine to run on Public Square was brought up but in 1861 it was amended to prohibit them in business section of city.

In 1862 the picket fence was put up—also around Monument Park.

In 1878 the Marshall was instructed to remove the fence, but the public objected.

By diplomacy the fence disappeared in one night in an unknown way, and a rumor had it that an Alpine Avenue farmer had a new fence along the front of his farm.

REED'S Lake Dummy line. By. Allye, Engineer.
Fare collected before you entered the car and cinders in your eye guaranteed.

THE first street cars ran from the head of Monroe Street to the old D. & M. depot in 1865.

Winegar's car line—Division Street to the Fair Grounds on Hall Street—started in 1873.

Jerry Boynton's line of cars in 1875 from Scribner Street, Bridge Street, past the City Hall and Post Office, Division, Monroe, and LaGrave Streets, out to the dummy line at Sherman Street to the lake.

—in 1885 all these lines consolidated.

THIS is the first Pavilion built at the end of the Dummy line at the Lake. Ice cream served in the main hall and a dining room for dinner parties showing at the left.

The present Ramona Pavilion is the third on this spot.

THE Owashtanong Club was organized in 1883 with down town club rooms.

In 1886 they built this boating and social club at the Lake—cost $12,000.00.

It was twice enlarged before the fire. Only the foundation ruins remain on the lake front.

Later, renamed as the Lakeside Club.

BOOZE and beer predominated around the end of the Dummy line at the lake so most of the family parties and Sunday School picnics were held at Miller's landing on the south shore.

THE first power boats on Reed's Lake could not carry large crowds, so in the picture you see Crook's barge, which had a parlor at one end, a bar at the other, and an open dancing floor center.

The two little steamers, Victor and Sport, would take turns in towing it out into the lake.

FROM the top of John St. hill, just back of the Masonic Temple, we have this view in 1865.

You can see the Henry, Kingsbury, and Lovell Moore homes at the left where the Press and Livingston Hotel buildings now stand.

Fulton Street Park shows in the center with its flag pole. The Congregational Church shows at the corner of Division and Monroe.

The later Park Congregational lot is empty and our Public Library and St. Cecelia buildings are yet to materialize.

LOUIS Campau's third home was at the top of Fulton Street hill—(now the Gay Home). When Campau's bank failed, he used the now-useless bank currency for wall paper in the tower room.

HENRY R. Williams, our first mayor, erected this stone house just above Crescent Park in 1851.

It was later occupied by Dr. Johnson and finally known as the Camp House.

This view was taken in the early sixties—showing a game of croquet in progress.

THE second High School was built just east of the old stone school and was completed in 1867—before the stone building was removed.

This, too, has gone, soon following the building of the Junior High School which is on the same location as the old stone building—though at a lower level.

A VIEW from near the top of Bridge Street hill.

The sand pile at the left later became Butterworth Hospital. The small German Church was replaced by the large brick structure.

The scaffolding is still on the schoolhouse that has long since been removed to make way for parking space.

In the distance you can see the lower two islands.

LOOKING down on some of the old mills just north of Bridge Street.

The flour mill near the bridge burned recently.

Seargant's and Sweet's big mills and the never fully completed stone church across the river show.

IN the early 50's the wooden West Side School was outgrown and the stone building was erected.

Built of river stone which cost only the hauling and labor at $1.00 per day of 10 hours.

The third floor was used for an Armory. A creek and swamp just to the west made a fine playground.

One winter the girls made a playground of a cave in the wood pile of 4-foot wood where the farmer had piled it hollow and saved a number of cords in his contract with the city.

The building condemned in 1872, and replaced by the Union High School.

LOOKING from the hill top above Sixth Street bridge, you can see the old curved dam in the river—built in 1849.

In 1866 the present dam was built farther south. You can see the lime kiln on the river's edge and much open space where our big factories are now busy.

LOOKING from the hill top toward Leonard Street bridge. The N. Ionia Street School in the foreground.

Behind the tower of the school is the old Tanner Taylor's Tannery—a stone building with a record of having four roofs burned off from it.

Just beyond is the Comstock Row. The big water works buildings and show case factories were not yet built.

C. C. COMSTOCK built the first multiple apartment dwelling in the city for the accommodation of the colored people who worked in his mills. You can see its location in the view above.

Below is a closer view showing the tenants driven out by the high water at the time of the big log jam, 1883.

LOOKING over the end of Reservoir Hill about 1865. The D. & M. Railroad bridge and depot were completed in the summer of 1858 and in July of that year the first steam train entered our city.

Three hotels show in the view.

Our city refused to grow toward the new station so for ten years busses made the mile and a half connection with the train's behind-time service, till the G. R. & I. came to the rescue of Campau's Town. The old depot is gone and, in acknowledgment of their mistake, the trains now back down the path the busses once took.

OUR city had many large losses by fire in the earlier days—but especially in the years 1872-3 and 4. The most extensive fire the city has had is shown in the accompanying picture. Much of the property between Canal Street and Ionia—north of Bridge Street— was burned. One hundred thirty families homeless and a number of mills destroyed. July 13, 1873.

THIS shows part of the buildings burned. Sweet's big mill is near the center of the picture.

Pearl and Bridge Street covered bridges show.

The two buildings on the right were not burned as you can see in the next view—after the fire.

LOOKING back over the ruins of the big fire.

The smoke is still rising from the ruins of Sweet's big mill.

SEVERAL woolen mills were in operation between 1845 and 1870.

This mill was built in 1857, operated by Allen P. Collar, Robert Hilton, and others—and burned October, 1868.

This is now the location of Bissell's Carpet-Sweeper factory.

The old toll bridge at Bridge Street shows behind the mill. The present cement bridge is the fifth one built at Bridge Street.

Part of the old Canal Basin shows in the foreground. This old water hole had a flavor all its own and the eastern half was filled in in 1849.

The building at the right was a cabinet shop, operated by Buddington and Thornton, located where the Bissell Carpet Sweeper offices are now.

This view was taken in 1865.

A VIEW of lower Canal Street—1860. The old Bronson House shows at the corner of Bronson (now Crescent St.).

Canal Street was paved with two rows of 8 ft. plank in 1854. Pearl to Bridge Street graded higher and paved with cobblestone as in this picture in 1859.

Again raised in 1872-3 to the present level.

Saengerfest Hall

GERMAN Musical Societies held their fourth convention here in August, 1881. There was no suitable hall for their purpose so they built this temporary structure on Lyon Street opposite the Empress Theater.

It had stage room for 400 singers—a tap room with steins around the walls—and ? % beer in kegs. Heroic size painted statuary of famous musicians adorned the roof edge.

Later the building was used for two political conventions, roller skating rink, and bicycle racing till a final finish came in one of the hottest fires the center of our city has experienced.

JUDGE George Martin, one of the early law-
yers, came here in 1836. He built his home on
the north sloping end of Prospect Hill. The
columned porch extended on three sides of the
house. This sketch was made in 1855 by Miss
Mary Cuming. The creek in the foreground is
now the City Hall site—and the barn back of the
house is close to our County Building. The
Norris Block just west of the City Hall replaced
this home many years ago.

*F*ourth of July, 1871. Parade of "Horribles" taken on
Lyon Street in front of the old County Building.

Judge Martin's home next, on the north tapering
end of Prospect Hill, through which Lyon Street, too,
was graded.

Mr. Chubb's house on the site of present City Hall.

HAVING completed our ramble—near the foot of Lyon Street hill, I have asked for one of the old Cable Cars with two trailers which are parked here, to take you home.

View, 1890.

Corrections and Updates

by James VanVulpen

Page 5 (bottom): As Fitch notes, this picture dates well before 1925. The "Vaudette" sign at extreme right narrows the time to around 1908 or '09.

Page 6: The general thrust of Fitch's explanation of downtown's odd street pattern is correct, but a few details should be noted. First, it couldn't have been much of a "race" to the land office — at White Pigeon, not Battle Creek or Kalamazoo — since Campau's purchase was made on September 19, 1831, and Lyon's on September 25, 1832, over a year later. (The Interurban Station, which stood on the Campau post site when Fitch wrote, was later replaced by the Welsh Civic Auditorium.) Old Louis's taunt to Lyon is probably apocryphal, but certainly expresses his intent. The first purchaser of lots 1 and 2 was Luther Lincoln, who erected his sawmill during the winter of 1833-34. He then sold out for a few hundred dollars to Abram Wadsworth, a speculator who turned a tidy profit by selling both lots and mill to Lyon's Kent Company for $5,500 in October 1835. The company's engineer, John Almy, then platted the land so Canal Street ran through to Pearl.

Page 9 (bottom): The muddy embankment in the foreground became the site of the Amway Grand Plaza tower in the early 1980s. The small wooden building — in which the town's first funeral parlor and undertaker supply business began in 1858 — stood where Israel's furniture store would be after 1976; Campau Avenue ran southward down the island's center. The Forslund condominiums stand almost entirely on land reclaimed from the river.

Page 10: The stone school was torn down in 1868, after its replacement was completed.

Page 12 (top): This picture was probably taken during the winter of 1887-88 (see page 15). The building actually got further religious use, being dismantled and rebuilt in the early 1900s out on Eastern Avenue for a Dutch congregation.

Page 13 (top): The view shows, further up Fountain, the cupola of Elias Matter's home which was built in 1871. This would probably place the photo in 1872.

Page 15 (top): A more likely date for this view would be the winter of 1887-88, as the tower of City Hall shows beyond the church, with its clock face not yet installed. It certainly wasn't there in 1875.

Page 15 (bottom): Mary McIntyre married Samuel Perkins on September 4, 1842. He died in 1866, and the widow refused all offers for the home, where she died in late 1913. Of their three sons, one died in infancy, the eldest, at age 43, hanged himself in the cellar of this house in 1890 and the youngest became a founder of the present American Seating Company. Date of the picture may be closer to 1910.

Page 17 (top): The typographical error in the second-to-last line should read, "before its removal in 1888," as correctly stated opposite.

Page 18: The four-story building partly blocking the view of the church was built in 1869 and still stands nearly 120 years later, owned and occupied by Dr. Robert J. Karl, Jr. This picture, then, probably shows later street work somewhere around 1870 and probably no later than '72, as the house at left was sold that year and turned to nonresidential use.

Page 19 (top): William Haldane's cabinet shop went up during the winter of 1836-37. The frame building was moved across the street in 1850, when Haldane erected this gothic cottage, and later moved again to the hill north of the Ball/Morton home, where it stood until 1888.

Page 19 (bottom): Three of the four buildings shown at the Ottawa-Pearl corner in 1925 still stood 60 years later, as did nearly all those showing in the distance. The exception, the Houseman Building visible at far left, was torn down in 1966.

Page 20 (top): Dr. Shepard wasn't quite the first doctor to arrive in Grand Rapids. Dr. Stephen Wilson beat him by two months, but died only four years later. Shepard lived until 1893 — in a house on the same Jefferson Avenue block as his longtime Prospect Hill neighbor, William Haldane.

Page 21: The present Morton House, the fourth hotel building to occupy this corner, was built in 1923 and converted to senior citizen housing in the 1970s.

Page 22 (bottom): Tolls were collected on sections of the plank road as fast as the sections were completed. Two to five stages a day were covering the route by summer 1854, when all but a seven-mile gap was planked. Even this "isthmus" was described as "far from being bad."

Page 24 (top): The Grand Rapids Trust Company structure, completed in 1926, is now the Michigan National Bank main office, topped by its famous weather ball.

Page 24 (bottom): The Grand Rapids Saving Bank, completed in 1916 on this corner, is now called the People's Building, at Ionia and Monroe Mall.

Page 25 (top): The correct date would be 1860, as Ball's bank wasn't begun until the winter of '59, and the trees beyond the completed are clearly in leaf. The cobblestone paving wasn't finished until '57. The Luce Block site would come to be known in the late 20th century as the "Wurzburg lot," subject of many plans for development.

Page 25 (bottom): The foreground cluster of buildings, all built after a fire in 1857 and before the Civil War, are among the oldest remaining downtown structures. They have recently undergone extensive interior renovation, but preserve much of their outer period charm.

Page 27 (top): The "present" Eagle Hotel of 1925, on the northwest corner of Market and Louis streets, closed during the Depression and was torn down in 1934, exactly 100 years after the original Eagle Hotel went up. A parking lot south of Kresge's dime store replaced the building until Monroe Avenue was cut through the block in 1978.

Page 27 (bottom): A plaque at the northeast corner of the Monroe amphitheater marks the spot where the Rathbun House once stood. The six-story Widdicomb Block replacement for the old structure was followed by the "art deco" Kresge dime store, which stood from 1936 to 1978.

Page 29 (top): The hardware store was originally a warehouse, built by James Watson on the riverbank at Fulton Street in 1834. It was moved up next to the Commercial Block in 1845, enlarged and remodeled into its final form.

Page 31 (bottom): Most of the buildings shown here stood some 60-plus years later. The Pantlind Hotel became part of the Amway Grand Plaza in 1981, a year after the Lovett Block across the street was remodeled into the Campau Square Building. The Grand Rapids National Bank — with 14 additional stories — became the McKay Tower. The Houseman store, with a new facade, was turned to other uses after that firm's removal in 1986, but the upper part of the onetime Fremont Block next to it continued to look much as it did when built in 1863.

Page 32: Since A.D. Rathbone died in 1856, and his son of the same name was only 17 in the summer of 1860, the man on the sidewalk is probably Amos Rathbone, a brother of the senior A.D.

Page 34 (top): Evidence, including store signs and the building under construction at extreme right, places the time of this photo as the spring of 1869. Most of these buildings survived to be restored by developers during the 1980s. The small wooden stores at left were replaced by Heman Leonard's three-story brick block in 1870; enlarged by another story in 1887 and given a white terra-cotta facade in 1912, it was occupied for many years by Houseman's clothing store.

Page 34 (bottom): Nearly every building in sight here was gone by the late 20th century. Sole exceptions were the two structure at right, south of Lyon Street. The corner one, erected in 1860, was occupied for over a century after 1883 by May's clothing store.

Page 35 (top): About 20 years after the jail's demolition in 1958, its site became a parking lot for the Oldtown Riverfront Building. The Tower Clock Building at Monroe and Pearl, which existed from 1875 to 1939, was replaced by a Woolworth dime store. The latter, after Monroe was extended south, was torn down in 1979 to make room for the mirror-sided Mutual Home Building and the parking garage west of it. Sweet's Hotel, a corner of which shows at right, later became the Pantlind.

Page 39 (top): The *Governor Mason* actually made its maiden voyage in the summer of 1837.

Page 39 (bottom): Fitch's account of the 1838 flood is fine — but the picture is of Pearl Street bridge on July 26, 1883, being battered by the rush of logs from the big jam.

Page 40 (top): The Island Park ballfield west of Market Avenue later was covered by city-owned buildings.

Page 41 (top): Summit Street later was renamed Ellsworth and still later took its final name from the avenue which extended from its southern end — Grandville.

Page 43 (bottom): The Porter Block occupied the old church lot from 1877 to 1947. Two years later the massive Herpolsheimer department store opened on the site. In 1985 Herpolsheimer's was remodeled into the City Centre shopping mall.

Page 44 (bottom): After this wooden building was torn down, the three-story brick South Division School stood on its site from 1884 to 1948. From the 1950s to the early 1980s, the location (255 South Division) was occupied by the Michigan Employment Security Commission office.

Page 45 (top): This fairground, sold in 1890 and platted into city blocks with lots zoned for residential and business purposes, formed the nucleus of the neighborhood known as Madison Square.

Page 45 (bottom): The onetime Campau farm, after years as a city park, was built up during the 1970s with government sponsored low-income housing units.

Page 46 (top): The Herald Building site is now a parking lot, and the Methodist church at the upper right was replaced by the Keeler Building, but the Peck drugstore "wedge" still stood well over a century later, occupied by the Revco drug firm which bought out Peck's.

Page 50 (top): The house at the upper left was on the Loraine Building site, not a block west, where stood the three homes Fitch mentions.

Page 50 (bottom): A plaque on the former Gay home's west wall commemorates the Campau house (the first built on Heritage Hill, incidentally) where Louis and Sophie lived from 1838 to 1862. After George Gay erected the present structure at 422 East Fulton in 1883, the old building was moved to the rear and used as a barn until it was torn down many years later.

Page 51 (top): In the late 20th century, the site of this stone house's east wing, at right in the photo, was occupied by Junior College's Spectrum Theatre.

Page 51 (bottom): Since it was first built upon, the southeast corner of Lyon and Ransom has always been used for educational buldings. This one was torn down in 1911, after the high school built just west of it in 1892 was converted into a junior high. The latter became Grand Rapids Junior College's east building in 1925, and on its site now stands the JC Learning Center.

Page 52 (top): In Fitch's day, Butterworth Hospital stood on the site now occupied by the hospital's nursing school and resident physician apartments; the present hospital was built across Bostwick Avenue in 1925. The North Division Avenue extension now runs through the schoolhouse lot.

Page 52 (bottom): The I-196 Gerald R. Ford Freeway, completed in 1964, runs from the photographer's vantage point just about through the center of this view.

Page 53 (top): This is another spot where four successive school buildings have stood. The 1875 Union High gave way in 1909 to the red brick Union building which later became West Middle School and still later became a community center.

Page 54 (bottom): The Comstock Row — or "Hotel d'Afrique," as insensitive individuals dubbed it upon its completion in 1872 — stood between the pumping station and the Number Five Fire Station sites.

Page 54 (top): In the way things have of coming full circle, the Grand Trunk Railroad (successor to the D. & M.) built a new yellow brick depot on the site of the old one in 1948 and abandoned its downtown station. Though its use for passenger traffic was brief, this building continued for many years to be used for handling freight and still stands at this writing.

Page 54 (bottom): The corner with smoke rising beyond it was the Hermitage Hotel site from 1888 to 1963, before the present Grand Rapids *Press* building covered the block.

Page 57: Over 120 years after this picture was taken, the north end of the Grand Center and the south end of the Justice Building filled the area shown.

Page 58 (top): Not a single structure in this view still exists. The wooden awning just north of the Bronson House marks approximately the spot where the Monroe Avenue entrance to the City-County Building complex has stood since 1969.

Page 58 (bottom): The site of Saengerfest Hall is now a parking lot, just west of the Waters Building.

Page 59: Both the Norris Block which succeeded Judge Martin's house, and Keith's Theater on the old County Building site, were demolished in the mid-1960s urban renewal to make room for the towering Old Kent Bank Building. In 1976, a few years after old City Hall was torn down, a Bicentennial time capsule was buried where Mr. Chubb's house once stood.

Page 60: Cable cars operated in the city only four years before the line was electrified in 1892. If the Street Railway Company had had the foresight to retain its cable on this one route, Grand Rapids' Lyon Street hill might today enjoy an aspect as picturesque as that of San Francisco. Well, almost.

The Past 60 Years

by *Gordon Olson*

Grand Rapids was preparing to celebrate its centennial when George Fitch wrote *Old Grand Rapids*. With a population of 130,000, Grand Rapids was Michigan's second largest city, identified by its furniture just as surely as Detroit was by the manufacture of automobiles. Dutch immigrants had made their mark on the city with their careful life styles, conservative business practices and Calvinist religion, but other groups had arrived in smaller numbers from all parts of Europe and also made their presence known.

Just as Fitch looked back at a city marked by dramatic change in its first 100 years, the same can be said for the six decades that have passed since the ink dried on his work. We are still the furniture city, but now it is to supply offices rather than homes that the furniture craftsmen labor.

The last streetcar clanged along Grand Rapids' streets over 50 years ago, and one passenger train — sustained in part by a government subsidy — serves where once there were 20 and 30 a day. Automobiles dominate city traffic, and air passenger travel, only an idea in Fitch's time, has become indispensable to his modern counterparts.

For Fitch and his friends, downtown Grand Rapids specialty and department stores were the focus of shopping forays. Mall was an unknown term, and suburbs were at the end of the streetcar lines. Were he to magically reappear today, Fitch would likely feel disoriented in today's larger, more diversely populated city. Ringed by suburbs, capable of communicating with an part of the world in seconds and no more than hours away from even the most distant places, the city — and its pace, people and landscape — would be markedly different to him.

A new generation has torn down and built over many of the landmarks most familiar to Fitch. But enough remains so that he would be able to find his way about most parts of the city, and after meeting and talking with today's residents, he would quickly discover a common bond: Like his generation, they are proud to call Grand Rapids home and eager to tell visitors of its virtues.

Fitch would also discover that his interest in historical photographs is shared by many today. Photographs from the Public Library, with additions from the Public Museum and Gerald R. Ford Museum, were used to update his work. He would be particularly pleased by the work of Godfrey Anderson. When urban renewal efforts were redefining the downtown landscape, Anderson carefully photographed the entire area. Now part of the Library collection, those views are an integral part of this book.

THE GRAND RAPIDS National Bank Building dominates Campau Square and downtown Grand Rapids in the late 1920s. Cars and streetcars compete for the roadway. Automobile drivers curse the bumpy car tracks and streetcar conductors take umbrage at drivers who dart across their path. This view seems to suggest that there are already more cars than parking spots.

THE PLACE TO begin a "ramble" through Grand Rapids is downtown, and the first thing we discover there is that a change is underway. It is 1935. Buses have replaced streetcars, tracks have been torn up, and Monroe Avenue is being repaved as part of a project designed both to make the area more attractive and to provide jobs for the unemployed.

COMPLETED, the street work provides a broad, smooth thoroughfare where automobiles and buses roll smoothly along, carrying thousands of shoppers and workers downtown each day.

BY THE 1950s, Monroe Avenue is "the strip," a place where teenagers cruise a regular circuit from Veterans Park to Monroe, down Monroe to either Lyon or Michigan, up the hill and then right on Ransom or Bostwick and back to the park to start again.

The scenes below, taken in 1979 and 1981, make it clear why there will be no more cruising. Monroe Avenue is now a mall. The buildings at its foot have been razed, and soon a foundation will flow where original settlers found fresh water springs. Although not as impressive as those found 150 years earlier, trees grow again in the heart of the city.

AS WE AMBLE toward Campau Square, our ear picks up the sound of band music. It is September 14, 1927, and the Grand Army of the Republic — Union Civil War veterans — has come to town. The veterans' numbers have dwindled, and their steps are taken more carefully, but as the *Grand Rapids Press* headline declares, "Lincoln's Army Marches Again."

LATER, A GROUP of the old soldiers, including Grand Rapids historian Charles Belknap (on the far right), posed for this group picture.

AS WE AMBLE through time, we take note of other groups on the streets. On more than one occasion, bands of volunteers are cleaning up the city. Armed with heavy machinery, this group seems especially determined to make a "clean sweep."

IN THE NEIGHBORHOODS, campaigns like this one organized by Lydia Brown, supplied tools and materials to anyone willing to help do away with debris and eyesores.

WE ALSO DISCOVER that a construction project is underway. Seeking to attract convention goers and employ the jobless as well, civic leaders have proposed the construction of a new convention center.

THE RESULT is an all-out campaign for a civic auditorium, and after voter approval of a bond issue during 1929, ground is broken and construction begun. During the dark early days of the Great Depression, the work provides welcome income for many Grand Rapids families. Here, City Manager George W. Welsh (left) poses with a group of workers.

AS WE CONTINUE our downtown walk, we quickly see that the Civic Auditorium is not the only local response to Depression hardships. Trucks are out collecting anything that can be sold, or repaired in city shops and reused. In city-run shops, workers repair items as varied as shoes and stoves. They are paid in city currency (scrip) that can be exchanged for goods and services. Hardly an ideal system, it is challenged in 1933 and dismantled as federal New Deal "alphabet" agencies are created.

THIS VIEW OF Grand Rapids from Crescent Park was taken in the 1890s, but in 1950 it still looked much the same. The Depression and two World Wars saw to that, but with the post-World War II recovery came opportunities for growth and change. Within a decade the towers of City Hall on the left and the County Building in the center will no longer dominate the view.

Downtown, looking along Lower Monroe south toward the Pantlind Hotel or north toward the Manger Hotel (which later becomes Olds Manor), we see a street dotted with 19th-century buildings that have been encrusted with 20th-century neon, plastic and aluminum. In the coming decade these structures will give way to new commercial and government office buildings.

BUILDINGS throughout the downtown area are experiencing the same fate. Smith's Opera House, at the southeast corner of Louis and Market, opened in 1885, served concert audiences and revival meeting participants for the next six decades before becoming the City Rescue Mission in its final years.

KEITH'S THEATER (originally the Empress), built in 1914 at a cost of $20,000, was located at Lyon Street and Bond Avenue. Described as one of the "most modern" theaters in the country at the time, it lasted until the 1960s when several blocks were leveled in the massive Lower Monroe Urban Renewal Project.

BEST KNOWN of all downtown buildings, and the one that rallied preservationists for a last-ditch salvation effort, was the City Hall. Opened amidst great fanfare in 1888, it was designed by Elijah Meyers, architect of Michigan's capitol building.

NO ONE was more ardent in the effort to save at least the City Hall clock tower than Mrs. Mary Stiles. Early on the morning the tower was scheduled for destruction, she chained herself to the wrecking ball and defied contractors to continue. This last, dramatic statement was abruptly brought to a halt when the ball was raised several feet in the air and Mrs. Stiles agreed to end her protest.

THE CONTROVERSY over City Hall marked the end, rather than the beginning, of the Urban Renewal Project. Some time before, a battalion of business and government officials had lined up to break ground for the future home of the Union Bank and Trust Building.

FOR OVER a decade, the area rocked to falling walls and was rolled under the onslaught of a new age.

PRIVATE AND publicly funded construction continued into the 1980s, and the magnitude of the last 25 years of change can best be seen from the air. In this 1981 aerial view, modern residents can identify the following buildings (from right to left): State, Frey, Union Bank, Grand Rapids Press, Federal, City Hall, County, Old Kent Bank, Calder Plaza, MichCon, Hall of Justice, Grand Center and Primebank. On the left, construction is beginning on the Grand Plaza Hotel.

BUT WE are getting ahead of our story. There are other parts of the city to visit before we end our ramble. East, up Michigan Street hill we go, turning around at the top to look back over the city. It is about 1960, and on our right is the Armory building, scene of many community gatherings and special events since its construction in 1916.

AS WE start down the hill, we glance back for a last look at another landmark building: the Grand Rapids (later Fox DeLuxe) Brewery. Here, at the corner of Michigan and Ionia, the last bottle of Grand Rapids beer was brewed in 1951. The abandoned building was razed 15 years later.

AS WE CONTINUE down the hill and get closer to the river, we decide to walk south and cross at the Fulton Street bridge. Part way across, and further back in time, we see an unusual site. It is 1931, and workers are clearing the river bottom, picking up debris and carrying stones to its banks. Later, they will install a series of low dams to stabilize the water level during dry summer months.

WE RETRACE our steps and decide to use the old Interurban bridge to cross the river. Pausing in the middle of our crossing, we look back at the Bissell Carpet Sweeper factory, a familiar downtown site since it was built in 1885. Further up the river where the Post Office now stands is the Grand Trunk depot.

AHEAD OF US on the west side are the familiar buildings of the Voigt Milling Company. By 1970, the mill is closed, and soon the buildings will be torn down. The block of concrete in the river at the left was once a support for the cable that ran from the west side power canal. It also served to break up ice flows in the spring.

TODAY, the area once occupied by the mill is the site of A-Nab-Awen Bicentennial Park and the Gerald R. Ford Presidential Museum. Those who were present will long remember the celebration that marked the opening of the Ford Museum, the Amway Grand Plaza Hotel and the Grand Rapids Art Museum during one triumphant week in 1981. The visiting dignitaries and gala events made for an occasion unparalleled in our community's history.

FURTHER OUT on the west side is an institution known to generations of Grand Rapidians. By the time of this 1909 photograph, John Ball Park is already a major summertime attraction. The elaborate formal gardens are gone, but its zoo, recreation areas, picnic areas and pavilion continue to draw visitors by the hundreds of thousands.

THE PARK'S attraction is as timeless as its statue of John Ball, the early settler and civic leader whose 40-acre bequest in 1884 started it all.

RESTING AT John Ball Park, we recall other recreation and entertainment features of our city. During the 1930s, when the economic situation seemed darkest, new facilities like the pool at Richmond Park were built with used materials by "scrip" laborers. No one was happier than the neighborhood kids.

A FEW YEARS later, spectators come to South High Field to see women's professional baseball. The Grand Rapids Chicks, playing a highly skilled brand of baseball before crowds as large as 10,000, are usually strong contenders for the All-American Girls Professional Baseball League crown, and win the championship in 1952.

DOWNTOWN, "Festival" has come to dominate early summer activities. Begun as an arts and crafts fair, its three days of food and entertainment attracts crowds beyond anyone's expectations. When this 1974 picture was taken, 100,000 people attended. In a few more years, crowds of half a million and more would flow from Calder Plaza onto the surrounding streets.

SYMBOL for Festival and the city, is *La Grande Vitesse*, the first outdoor sculpture in the nation to built with a combination of private gifts and federal funding. Its design was criticized by many, and construction was closely watched and commented upon.

ON THE east side of the city, Ramona Park undergoes its share of change. In 1934 the Mystic Chute and Derby Racer rides attract thousands each weekend, Kruizenga's Garden is a popular retreat and Charles Poisson's *Ramona* takes passengers on leisurely Reeds Lake cruises. For the more active there is the Ramona Cycle Club, with riding activities sponsored by the Boston Store.

THE Ramona Pavilion was torn down in 1949, and the amusement park closed five years later. Today, sailboats have replaced the *Ramona,* and the lofty spire of the Mayflower Congregational Church dominates the horizon.

OUR RAMBLE has taken us to nearly all parts of the city, as we have moved back and forth over six decades. Now, resting from the long walk, our thoughts turn to the transportation revolution the city has seen. It is hard to believe that the city's first regularly scheduled air passenger service was inaugurated on July 31, 1926. Or that 20 years later Senator Arthur Vandenberg would mark two decades of passenger service by boarding an airliner for the postwar Foreign Ministers Conference in Paris.

AIR TRAVEL gets the attention, but before 1950 it is the Union Railroad Depot on Ionia Avenue, built in 1900 (and razed in 1961 for a freeway ramp) that greets most new arrivals and sends local residents on their journeys.

EASILY AS significant as the growth of air travel is the construction of the freeway system that speeds millions of people in and out of the city and to all parts of the nation each year. North-south and east-west freeways become corridors through the city and at the same time barriers to movement within it. In the course of freeway construction, numerous distinctive buildings, such as the octagon house on Michigan hill and the stone and brick structure at 337 Bridge Street, are razed.

TO END OUR ramble and historical musings, we head back downtown along Fulton Street. Close in, at La Grave Avenue, is the building that originally housed Oliver Bleake's general store in the 1850s. By 1930 it is the Doll House, and later it becomes the home of the West Michigan Tourist Association. Behind it stands the well-known Cottage Bar that first opened its doors in 1927.

HEADING WEST on Fulton, we glance to our right for a look at the distinctive Ryerson Library built in 1904. In front of the building is a 1939 parking sign that brings a nostalgic yearning for the good old days from any modern driver.

FURTHER ALONG, at the southwest corner of Fulton and Sheldon is the Grand Rapids *Press* headquarters, and at the right edge of the photograph can be seen the last remnants of the *Herald* building, closed after the death of the *Herald* in 1959. Now, a parking lot stands on the site.

PAST THE NEWSPAPER buildings on the southwest corner of Fulton and Division stands the Cody Hotel. Built in 1887 as the Warwick, its name was changed in 1893 by owner Darwin Cody, cousin of the famous, "Buffalo Bill." Its days are numbered when this 1950s photo is taken; torn down in 1958, it was replaced four years later by a parking ramp.

IT IS TIME TO END our journey, and there is no better place to do that than the Public Museum at State and Jefferson. There, thanks to the restored Calkins Law Office, and the Gaslight Village, we can step back in time to the city's earliest days. Like a living history textbook, these displays are a bond between the small village of 150 years ago and today's modern urban center.